IMAGES OF ENGLAND

THE CITY OF
COVENTRY

IMAGES OF ENGLAND

THE CITY OF
COVENTRY

GRAHAM KEMPSTER

TEMPUS

Frontispiece: The old favourite – the Golden Cross dates back to the times of Henry VII. It stands in the oldest part of the city near the old County Hall and former jail, the ruins of the old cathedral and St Mary's hall. The inn is half-timbered with three fine gables. The ceilings, both upstairs and downstairs, are in old English oak and the cellars cut out of the sandstone rock on which the inn stands. Various organisations have used the inn as a meeting place and most notable was the Golden Cross philanthropic society, a group of people who always showed great enterprise in their fundraising. They were probably the first organisation to bring a flying display to Coventry in 1913, and when hard times threatened citizens after the First World War, a Christmas parcel fund was started and 500 joints of meat and batches of groceries were given away. At one time, the inn was the headquarters of Coventry and Warwick's Football League. Chef & Brewer now own it.

First published 2004

Tempus Publishing Limited
The Mill, Brimscombe Port,
Stroud, Gloucestershire, GL5 2QG
www.tempus-publishing.com

British Library Cataloguing in Publication Data.
A catalogue record for this book is available from the British Library.

ISBN 0 7524 3357 1

Typesetting and origination by Tempus Publishing Limited.
Printed in Great Britain.

Contents

Acknowledgements

Many thanks to June Fairbrother, Chief Librarian at the *Coventry Evening Telegraph*, whose professional and local knowledge helped to make the compilation of this book a lot easier.

Special thanks to Alan Kirby, Editor of the *Coventry Evening Telegraph*, for allowing access to his newspaper's archives.

Introduction

Coventry is a proud city of spires steeped in centuries of history. It is renowned throughout the world, not least for the Blitz bombing of the Second World War which devastated the city but gave birth to a new beginning and a new hope. A wonderful new cathedral stands proudly alongside the ruins of the old and Coventry is now recognised as an international centre of reconciliation.

Hitler's bombs cost many lives and decimated major areas, particularly the city centre. From the rubble, a pioneering new pedestrianized shopping precinct was built and today another huge phase of development is underway to transform the central area. On the outskirts of the city, the skyline is also changing as the fantastic new arena project takes shape, creating an entertainment and conference centre and new home for the Coventry City football club, the Sky Blues.

Ribbon-making, the manufacture of machine tools and, more latterly, telecommunications have been prominent in Coventry's industrial history and today high technology businesses work hand-in-hand with the local Coventry and Warwick universities.

Above all, it is the motor industry that has dominated Coventry's industrial heritage. Local cycle manufacture ultimately led to the development of the motorised vehicle and since that time, generations of Coventry families have helped design and build famous makes. Thousands are still employed by Jaguar, Peugeot and the famous black cab company London Taxis International.

It was a legendary horse ride by a naked Lady Godiva in protest at local taxes which probably brought most notoriety to Coventry. A statue in her memory stands proudly in the heart of the city centre and, with the chiming of a nearby clock, Peeping Tom sneaks a naughty look at her exquisite figure to the delight of tourists and shoppers.

The photographs in this book remind us of the city's proud heritage. Most are from the archives of the *Coventry Evening Telegraph*, the local daily newspaper which has served the people of Coventry since 1891.

Alan Kirby (Editor, *Coventry Evening Telegraph*)
June 2004

A view from the top of Bishop Street in the 1950s. The two spires and the Owen Owen building dominate in the distance.

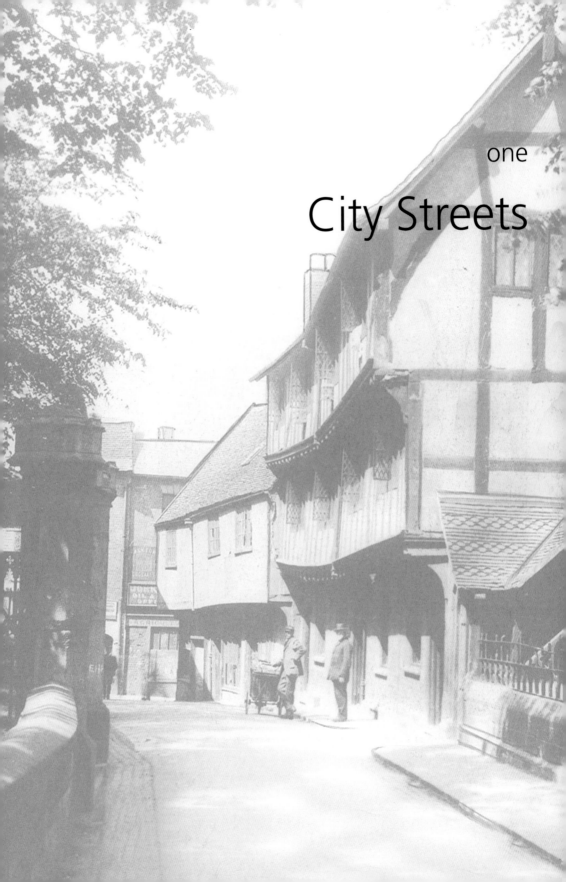

one

City Streets

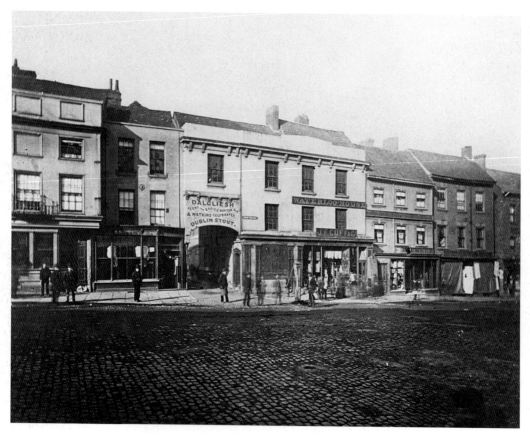

In medieval times, Broadgate led to the 'Broad Gate of the Earl's Castle' – hence its name. It was a busy, narrow thoroughfare with street markets and increasing horse traffic. In 1921, ancient buildings were demolished to facilitate a considerable widening of Broadgate. In this photograph from the 1860s, above the 'Dalgliesh' hoarding, the Broad Gate street sign can be seen and, to the right of the hoarding on the Waterloo House building, is the Cross Cheaping street sign. As photography was a rare enterprise at this time, the man with the camera is causing much interest. The ghostly human images we can see are the onlookers who have moved during the long exposure necessary to record the scene.

A further photograph of Broadgate from the 1860s, this time at the junction with Smithford Street. On the right, with ironwork verandas, is the Coventry Hotel and in the centre of the picture on the corner of Hertford Street, Peeping Tom can be seen looking down from his window above Piggott's boot & shoe warehouse. Twentieth-century traffic made the crossroad more and more crowded and, in the years before the Second World War, the weekends were a nightmare for both road users and pedestrians alike. After the Blitz, vast changes took place in the appearance of Coventry's 'Top of the Town'.

A slightly later view of Broadgate, possibly from the 1880s or '90s, showing the street market extending out into the road. In the background are the Standard Printing Office and shops to the right, of which Dalgliesh now has a more sober frontage. At Waterloo House, A. Adcock & Co. Telegraph Office has taken over from J.F. Cuff & Co.

Broadgate looking towards Cross Cheaping at 11 a.m. on 29 November 1929 – Armistice Day – when traffic came to a standstill and the crowd observed a moment's silence. In the middle of the road stand PC 150, Smith, and Inspector Langford. The buildings advertising Mitchells & Butlers and Gilbey's would soon be pulled down to make way for the new Owen Owen store.

Broadgate by night in 1937, showing Owen Owen's new store and Trinity Street, both newly completed. Owen Owen's store was destroyed in the air raids of the Second World War. At the time that this photograph was taken, H. Samuel occupied the same premises as seen in the previous picture but, next door to them, Mansfields have taken over from Slingsby.

This pre-war photograph shows the shops leading up to the National Provincial building. They include Hayward & Son the outfitters, Newton's the drapers (with a café above), J. Lyons' teashop and Sketchley Dyeworks. Next to them is Kendall's, which sold umbrellas and raincoats. On the floor above them is the dentist, C. Angus and, on the next floor, a life assurance company together with the Casson Dancing School. The last recognisable business belongs to the City Shirt Shop. With the exception of the bank building which was incorporated into the new city centre, the whole square was demolished during an eleven-hour air raid on 14 November 1940. The tramlines carrying the public transport system were abandoned shortly after the raid due to the enormous expense entailed in relaying the track over miles of the city.

Looking towards the National Provincial Bank (now NatWest) in Broadgate, a year before the Coventry Blitz. Outside Boots the Chemist, the *Coventry Evening Telegraph* news vendor's headline announces 'Lords Rush Through IRA Bill'. Today's motoring enthusiasts will recognise a wealth of different pre-war vehicles in the street. H. Samuel's distinctive clock can be seen, then Alexandre the tailor's and, on the corner of Market Street, is A.D. Wimbush, the tobacconist.

Overleaf: Through the generosity of Coventry-born Mr Bassett-Green and the fine artistry of Sir William Reid Dick, the twentieth-century equestrian figure of Lady Godiva stands in the garden island of Broadgate. This picture shows the unveiling of the statue by Mrs Lewis Douglas, the wife of the American ambassador to the Court of St James, on 22 October 1949.

Above: Old grammar school corner in Hales Street, looking towards Well Street, 1927. The grammar school building dates back to the fourteenth century and was converted into a grammar school by John Hales in the sixteenth century. It served its purpose until 1885 when the school was moved to Warwick Road. On the corner of Well Street, facing the camera, is A.C. Stenson's wine lodge, advertising 'Truman Hanbury Buxton & Co, London Stout'. When Corporation Street was constructed in the 1930s, new premises were built on the corner of the Burges. The pub is now The Tally Ho. Displayed in the window is a poster for a production of *Midnight Molly*. Next door is W.H. Crofts, the purveyor of fish, game and poultry.

Opposite above: Broadgate photographed in 1958 from the tower of Holy Trinity church, showing three completed sides; the bridge really was a bridge, the island was a garden to be proud of, and the traffic went round and round. The building in the bottom left of the picture comprised the iron-roofed temporary shops facing Broadgate island.

Right: This unusual photograph, taken from almost the same spot as the previous picture, shows what appears to be an army recruiting march. Soldiers in uniform are leading a number of flat-hatted civilians. There is no date on the photograph, but a good guess would be some time between the wars.

Below: Demolition begins at the junction of Hales Street and the Burges in 1930. Its destruction enabled the formation of Corporation Street to go ahead.

Above: A wonderfully clear picture of Hertford Street around 1910 with Warwick Lane to the right and the junction of Bull Street to the left. Hertford Street was a new city street in 1812 when it was built to accommodate the growing coach and carriage traffic in the direction of Warwick. It replaced Greyfriar's Lane and Warwick Lane which were described as narrow and dangerous. Peeping Tom is seen peering down from his window. In the bottom window of the same building, a Coventry Hippodrome flyer announces Leonard Mortimer in *The Little Captain*. On the opposite side of the road are the premises of Curtis & Beamish, printers and stationers. Further down the street are the prominent Geisha Café sign (the Geisha was still in business in the '60s), the Coventry Ribbon House, and Haddon's sports shop and haircuttting rooms. The picture also shows the changing face of transport with trams, horse-drawn carriages and an early motor car all in evidence at the same time.

Opposite above: Fleet Street, between Hill Street and Smithford Street, was due for demolition to make way for the new Corporation Street when it was photographed in 1929. Apart from the Coventry and District Dairy Co.'s premises, the shops are empty and the businesses transferred. Just visible on the windows to the right and the corner of the archway are Coventry Corporation's 'condemned buildings' notices.

Opposite below: Warwick Lane in 1939. Grapes Inn was at the bottom of the lane between Cramps the tobacconists and Taylor's the sports car specialists. The Grapes was originally outside the city wall. However, when civil war raged and Coventry was threatened by a second attack from King Charles I, so citizens uprooted the Grapes along with other timber-framed buildings and re-erected them inside the wall. It stood on this site in Warwick Lane until high explosive bombs demolished it during the Second World War, but it was opened again in the stores of the former building to fill a gap in the lives of its customers! Above Simon's grocery shop is an advertisement for Nestlé's milk and a poster for the Opera House, announcing that the Coventry Repertory Co. would be presenting Benn W. Levy's comedy, *This Business Woman*, twice nightly at 6.30 p.m. and 8.50 p.m. from Monday 20 February 1939.

This picture of Hertford Street was taken opposite the Coventry Ribbon House. A man can be seen looking longingly at a window display which is full of Coventry-made Rudge Whitworth cycles – 'Britain's Best Bicycle' – priced at £4 4s 6d. Above the shop, Wilson's dental surgery offers 'painless extractions' for one 1s. Next door is the chemist, R. Evan Parker, sharing a shop entrance with Beaver & Co., the photographers. Behind the head of the man in the straw boater is a sign for 'Fletcher's Artificial Teeth'. Haddon's hairdressers and sports shop is showing a window display of tennis racquets and a sign over the door advertises 'singeing'.

This is how Hertford Street looked in 1929. Peeping Tom's building has changed hands from H.E. Willford to S.W. Turner. Gone are the lovely ornate ironwork verandas, a door has replaced the corner window, and the lower section of the building appears to have been tiled over. Further down the street, the wall signs for the Geisha Café, Wilson's dental surgery, and Haddons have disappeared, but a huge hairdressing hoarding has been erected at roof level. Curtis & Beamish still occupy their premises on the corner of Warwick Lane. Halfway down Hertford Street on the right is the sign for Luckman's pianoforte warehouse. They occupied 58-59 Hertford Street and were agents for Allison, Chappell and Steinway Pianos. They also had the agencies for Columbia and HMV records and gramophones. Their telephone no. was 3890. The business was taken over by Hanson's music shop in the 1930s.

Above: Johnson and Mason, the wine and spirit merchants of Broadgate and Pepper Lane, acquired these imposing buildings in Hertford Street from Wyley & Co., the chemical manufacturers, and opened their business in 1885. This picture dates from around that time. The building accommodated a double-fronted shop and a sumptuously appointed suite of offices. Beer, wine and spirits were decanted from scores of giant casks.

Opposite above: The King's Head hotel on the corner of Hertford Street and Smithford Street in 1929, with excavations beginning for the foundations of the National Provincial Bank (now NatWest). The King's Head was one of the most extensive and well-appointed hotels in the Midlands; its windows, for example, were filled with stained glass illustrating scenes from bygone Coventry. It opened in 1879 on the site of the old hotel, the Red Lion. In the upper storey, there is an effigy in the corner of Peeping Tom. In 1939, an IRA bomb exploded in Broadgate, shattering the windows of the row of shops on the ground floor of the hotel. These included Dunn & Co., Allen's, and Statham & Fensom. The hotel was completely destroyed in the bombing of 14 November 1940. The bank survived and is the only remaining pre-war building in Broadgate. The building to the left of the King's Head is the Empire Theatre.

Opposite below: The Geisha Café in Hertford Street in 1961 offered a choice of self-service or waitress service. Barratt's, the fruiterers and florists, were next door. Further along the street is Brightwall's the army stores; Carvells ladies' and gentlemen's hairdressers; W.H. Smith; Holbrooks and the Church Bookshop. The bookshop proprietor was John Collier who died in 1981.

Butcher Row in the days before the First World War. It was known to have been in existence for 500 years, butchers would congregate in its narrow cobbled way to slaughter pigs and cattle. When this picture was taken, the butchers had long gone and the shops had been taken over by home furnishers and antique dealers.

Looking the other way along Butcher Row. The huge sign leaves us with no doubt as to who is trading from this shop! On sale are a 'cheap bedstead, 4s 6d, cheap' and what appears to be an ornate mirror for 16s 6d. In the background, Hilton's Booterie advertises 'England's Best'.

Right: Butcher Row a few years on. William Franks, selling furnishings and three-piece suites from the pavement, used a number of the shops for many years.

Below: The last days of Butcher Row. Shortly after this picture was taken, the Row was officially closed by the Mayor, Alderman Charles Payne, on New Years Day 1936. Butcher Row was demolished to make way for the construction of Trinity Street to ease the traffic flow to Broadgate. Until that time any vehicles travelling from the north of the city had to use Hales Street and the Burges. The demolition contractor for Butcher Row was Eli Pearson who also demolished Warwick Gaol. Many of the old timbers were stored for use in the future renovation of old buildings but during the invasion scare of 1940 the timbers were used to build obstacles on the partly finished A45. After the Second World War, the old timbers mysteriously disappeared!

Little Butcher Row looking towards Cross Cheaping in about 1910. Records of the street's existence date back to the fifteenth century. The tall half-timbered building sold antiques and bric-a-brac, and next door to its left is the bakery of J. Nassau. Nearest to the camera, the provision merchant W. Bird has a window-full of half sides of meat. On the window is advertising for 'Fry's Pure Cocoa'. The photographer has attracted an audience of local children; while the boys are striking various, almost staged attitudes – Artful Dodgers all – the little girl stands nicely with her hands behind her back.

Above left: Little Butcher Row in the 1920s. W. Bird's shop has changed hands and the building next door has had a glass shop-front added. A tradesman's sign hangs above the shop, but it is unclear what it might represent. The former bakery building has been extensively altered with a flat roofline and six large windows.

Above right: Almost gone. Little Butcher Row during the last stages of demolition in 1936. Who the young lady is, and why she is posing in front of the rubble, is unknown.

Night descends on the city. This picture of Trinity Street is on a wet evening in November 1952; the lights from the shops and offices reflect in the rain-soaked road.

Opposite above: The demolition continues. Old properties are being pulled down to clear a path for Trinity Street. The Hippodrome can be seen on the left.

Opposite below: Demolition in 1962 of property alongside the central fire station in Hales Street has changed the appearance of this area at the bottom of Trinity Street. From this point the main block of the Lanchester College of Technology and more of the cathedral to the right can be seen. A proposal was made to convert the site to a temporary car park for 200 vehicles, and then use the land for the construction of a new road linking the Hales Street-Trinity Street junction with Cox Street at a future date. Also proposed was a new bus station on the north side of the road, a skating rink and the replacement of the central fire station with new premises in the Godiva Street area.

This new junction was constructed in 1967 to enable traffic from Hales Street to cross Trinity Street into Fairfax Street. Coventry fire brigade had their own control button in the central fire station to alter the traffic signals and clear the way for appliances in the event of an emergency call being received. The main reason for opening the new road through the island was to bring Fairfax Street into greater use, as Ford Street was to be closed when work started on stage five of the Inner Ring Road.

Opposite: A view of a damp Trinity Street during the rush hour seen from the roof of the Owen Owen building in September 1960. The traffic is two-way and cars are parked everywhere, even in the middle of the road. The Coventry Theatre rises out of the gloom in the distance.

The traffic weaving up Trinity Street in 1964 is complicated on a busy Saturday by the number of people crossing the street and using the centre refuge. Trinity Street traffic's weaving progress was a result of the one-way traffic system in this part of the city centre. Traffic entering the street from one side of Hales Street had to cross if going up to Broadgate, and traffic entering from the other side had to cross if following the one-way system around Ironmonger Row.

In the severe weather conditions of January 1968, Corporation bus crews lend a hand to push cars stuck in Trinity Street so the buses can continue on their way. A surprise overnight blizzard left 9in of snow, disrupted bus services, trapped cars, and meant thousands had to walk to work. Production came to a standstill at Pressed Steel Fisher and Jaguar, and five miles of traffic leading towards Coventry soon built up at Stonebridge.

This historic photograph of the High Street dates from the 1860s and is thought to have been taken by Mr Wingrave whose chemist's shop can be seen on the corner of Pepper Lane. This Elizabethan building was restored in the 1930s and, in the years before the war, was the premises of Harrison's the opticians. Unfortunately, it was a victim of the 1940 air raid. The building with the carriage outside housed the tea and coffee merchants, Atkins and Turton, and later became a branch of Martins Bank. It survived the war and for some years was occupied by Coventry Building Society before being demolished for the redevelopment of Broadgate in the 1990s.

The High Street in the 1920s. To the left is the Craven Arms, now the site of Barclays Bank, and in the distance at the top of Broadgate is the Coventry Arms, which was demolished in 1928. The tenant at that time was Walter Newman.

With the Coventry Arms demolished, the King's Head hotel could be seen from this area, as is evident in this 1930s photograph. It is interesting to note the position of the 'Iron Jelloids' sign way up above the pavement; it is not exactly in the line of sight.

The steps and columns of the National Westminster Bank give the location of this scene away. Taken in about 1936, the corner shop with the Broadgate address is the tobacconists, Salmon and Gluckstein, who sold Barn 81 cigars: five for 2s 6d, twenty-five for 12s, and fifty for 23s 6d. The Glove Shop has a sale, and next door is Martins Bank. Harrison's the opticians are on the other side of Pepper Lane.

A new traffic island at the Broadgate junction in 1955. Compare this picture with the previous one and it can be seen that whilst the Martins Bank building remained standing after the war, the buildings on either side were destroyed. A Blindell's van is parked outside the flat-roofed shops on the other side of Pepper Lane where the ancient building that housed Harrison's once stood.

High Street seen from Broadgate in 1963.

Right: Jordan Well in 1941. In 1410, the name applied only to a well but by 1421 the street had adopted the name. The central shop in the picture is A. McCutchion & Son who sold fresh greengrocery and wet fish. Shoppers would queue from as early as 5.30 a.m. when food was short after the First World War in case the farmers delivering fruit and vegetables brought any rabbits. Kids at the time would help unload the wagons of cabbages and swedes in return for wages of around 2d.

Below: Jordan Well in 1959. With the development of the Herbert art gallery and museum and the expansion of Lanchester College of Technology, this block of old shopping property was soon to be demolished. McCutchion's were still trading from the same spot and, alongside them, was Osborne's newsagents and tobacconists with posters for Weights cigarettes, Bachelor tipped at 3s 4d for twenty, and *The Daily Herald* – 'Britain's Friendliest Newspaper'. On the other side of McCutchion's is the men's outfitters L.A. Ghent. At the end of the row, over the shop with 'sale' above the window, is a large banner proclaiming 'This building is coming down; all stock must be cleared, no reasonable offer refused'.

The changing face of Jordan Well in 1961 when the medieval row of shops in the previous photographs had been demolished for the expanding Lanchester College. This view from the top of the college shows work underway on clearing the site for the new tutorial block. It was to be a low building stretching from Jordan Well to Cope Street housing departments for electrical engineering, applied physics and maths, and part of the chemistry, metallurgy and textile sections. The white narrow building to the right of the Gaumont cinema is the Godiva Café.

Opposite: In 1967, the building housing the ladies' hairdressers at 40 Jordan Well was identified as part of a fourteenth-century 'hall house'. In its earliest days, the building would have been heated by an open-hearth fire, the smoke escaping through a hole in the roof. The central hall with bays at either end would have opened to the rafters. This unique building was considered for inclusion in the Spon Street townscape scheme. Just to the right of the salon was a tobacconists and sweet shop selling Capstan and Cadets cigarettes; notice the 1d YZ chewing gum machine on the wall.

Bishop Street in 1862. Bishop Street dates back to the twelfth century and was an important thoroughfare containing tradesmen's dwellings and, as can be seen, several substantial houses.

Bishop Street in the 1920s. On the corner with Well Street are Fearis & Co., the provisions merchant and confectioner. On the other side of the Truman's pub is J. Boswell the butcher's, and Waters' restaurant; these were all later demolished to make way for Corporation Street.

An unusual view of St Michael and Holy Trinity church spires as seen from the top of Bishop Street. The policeman on point duty is carrying his tin helmet, making this a wartime photograph. Sadly many of the streets' fine houses were lost in the war.

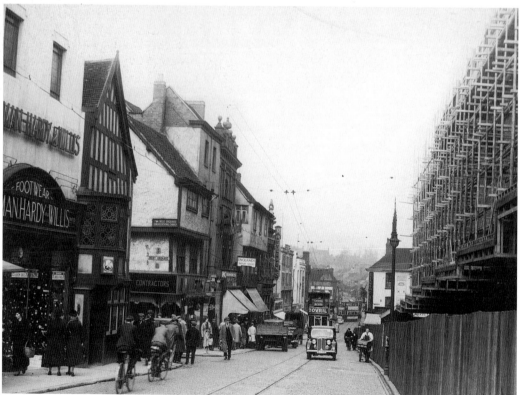

Above: Owen Owen's store is complete. This 1939 picture shows the contrast between the old buildings on the unchanged side of the street, and the modern architecture on the other. The department store was destroyed in the bombing of 1940.

Opposite above: Cross Cheaping dates back to the thirteenth century – the word 'cheaping' formerly referring to a market. In medieval times, the stalls spread out into neighbouring streets even as far as St Michael's churchyard. There were fishmongers' and leather sellers' stalls in the Cheaping itself. In 1541, a magnificent cross was erected at a cost of £200; a replica of this can be seen near the Cathedral Lane's shopping development. The street was finally closed to traffic in 1952 during work on the new Owen Owen store. This photograph was taken in 1932. On the left is Hurrells shop sign, Timpsons, the Canadian Fur Co., and Freeman Hardy & Willis are further down. The no. 5 tram has a red triangle on a white background indicating its route was Allesley Road to Bell Green. It advertises Savage's famous bread. The shops to the right would soon be pulled down for the new Owen Owen store.

Opposite below: This photograph of Cross Cheaping looks towards the Burges in 1936. The construction of the Owen Owen store is well underway. On the other side of the street, little has changed. Freeman Hardy & Willis stands next to the old Talbot Inn, then West Orchard with its sign to the Congregational church, then Milletts and Mattersons.

Right: Smithford Street. Originally known as Smythes Ford, it dates from the twelfth century, and was so named because the ford across the River Sherbourne was much used by smiths. English drama was cradled in this thoroughfare – it was the setting for the Coventry mystery plays and royalty came to see them. It was also the birthplace of arguably one of England's greatest actresses, Dame Ellen Terry. In May 1957, the last shop, Marlow's furniture and radio shop, closed and moved round the corner into Smithford Way. In this picture, Peeping Tom can be seen in his window over Piggott's boot and shoe warehouse on the corner of Hertford Street. The cobbled road to the right is Broadgate.

Below: Smithford Street was full of bustle and charm right up to its destruction in the Coventry air raids. Cookes, the tobacconists, and Arthur Francis, the drapers, are shown in the centre of this Edwardian picture.

A busy day in Smithford Street during the Second World War. The horse-drawn delivery wagon on the left carries the morale boosting message: 'Your courage, your cheerfulness, your resolution will bring us victory'. British Home Stores contains an ARP shelter for 330 people and a sign on Woolworths' opposite points the way.

Left: The name Much Park Street refers to the big park at Cheylesmore owned by the Black Prince in the middle of the fourteenth century. The street was the first packhorse road, then the main stagecoach route to London. During the 1940 Blitz, many old buildings were destroyed but some of medieval timber-framed properties that remained intact became the subject of a controversial scheme to remove them to Spon Street as part of the townscape project. The property seen here in Much Park Street was due for demolition in 1957 because of the danger of falling bricks, whilst Kensitas, Park Drive and Senior Service were on sale.

Below: Much Park Street in 1959. The New Star public house stands to the right and beyond on the same side of the street is the building where the first standard cars were made in 1903. At a later date, Charlesworth Bodies were made there, then Lea Francis Cars. Much Park Street is now the approach to Coventry's law courts.

These centuries old timber-framed houses in Much Park Street have been marred in appearance by modifications and the depredations of time. Nos 7–10 were to be pulled down and reconstructed in Spon Street.

The demolition in 1962 of the condemned former cycle shop G. Stokes & Co. and a café known as the Dew Drop Inn in Much Park Street had laid bare these heavy oak beams, massive blocks of local sandstone and the wattle and daub of which they were built in about 1400. Originally, the two properties were medium-sized hall houses with open hearths.

Opposite: Trinity Lane in the late 1920s. This was known as Cuckoo Lane in 1353 and in 1675 marked the boundary between the parishes of St Michael and Holy Trinity. These historic buildings were demolished in 1933 to make way for Trinity Street. In the background the cottages in Priory Row can be seen.

Above: Priory Row around 1900. As late as 1815, Priory Row was known as 'the lane withoutside St Michael's churchyard'. The lane probably existed in medieval times because it formed the boundary between the Earl's half and the Prior's half. Before 1807, it made a detour to the Bishop's Palace, avoiding the gardens, but was straightened at some point to give access to the new St Michael's burial ground. This picture shows the half-timbered buildings built during the middle of the sixteenth century. Nos 3, 4 and 5 of the cottages were originally Lych Gate House erected by John Bryan, who was the vicar of Holy Trinity. The cottage beyond was built at a later date and stood on the corner of Butcher Row. To the right of the picture are the gates of the Blue Coat School, founded in 1714. It was the first charity school for girls in Coventry and its home in Priory Row still exists. The school took pupils for two or three years and often the girls were trained for domestic service. Butchers Row is visible at the end of Priory Row.

Left: Looking the other way along Priory Row.

The Greyfriars Green in the Warwick and Queen Row areas was known as Cheylesmore Green in the early nineteenth century. Where the statue of Sir Thomas White stands was a large pit of water and tradition has it that it was used for ducking unruly women. Before it was enclosed by iron railings, boys played cricket there, and prior to 1858, it also hosted the Great Fair. In 1875 the Green was awarded to the Corporation. On the west side, Queens Road was called Summerland Butts until 1887 and by 1882 houses of a superior character were being built. This view appears to have been taken on a warm day in the early 1900s.

This summer stroll was photographed on 27 August 1933. Enjoying the weather, they are passing the spot where the men in the previous picture were enjoying their day in the sun on the grassy area. A First World War tank now stands in the same place, surrounded by iron railings.

Left: Somewhere in the vicinity of this overgrown ditch in Priory Row is the reputed grave of Lady Godiva and Earl Leofric. Godiva's legendary ride may be no more than fable but there is no doubt that she was a great benefactor of the city. The stonework in the picture is part of the foundations of the enormous St Mary's priory, which she endowed. More of the foundations were uncovered during the building of the new cathedral. This area, the highest ground within the city walls, is thought to have been the focal point of religious activity since the founding of the first settlement at Cofa's Tree.

Right: A Corporation stonemason is at work in 1949 restoring the foundations of the Benedictine priory and rebuilding the wall of Blue Coats school to its original size.

Corporation Street, at one time Coventry's worst accident blackspot. A check by the West Midlands' county council in the 1980s showed that there had been twenty-four accidents causing injury in three years. The figures applied to the length of road from the Burges to Hill Street but transport chiefs were especially concerned about the Hill Street junction, pictured here on the left just beyond the pelican crossing.

Shops along Corporation Street in 1972 included, from the left, Gibb's electrical goods showroom which opened in 1968 under the management of David Cooksey; Asher's curtain fabric shop which began life as a stall in Coventry market in the 1920s by Simon Asher; further down, is the Sleep and Lounge Centre with three large showrooms covering the ground, first and second floors.

Corporation Street in 1959. Opened in 1931, the street relieved considerable traffic pressures on other central roads. Some bus services, which had previously used Smithford Street, were diverted along it. The new gas and electricity showrooms were opened near the wine lodge. In 1937, Alderman Barnacle opened the Philpot circuit Rex cinema. It was bombed in the 1940 air raids. The Coventry and district Co-op rebuilt its store fronting Corporation Street and opened in 1954. This photograph shows the Belgrade Theatre, which was opened by the Duchess of Kent in 1958, and the *Coventry Evening Telegraph*'s new premises which were completed in 1959 when the offices were transferred from Hertford Street.

two

Markets

In 1867, the city's market hall with its tower and public clock was opened to the public and street stalls were finally swept away from Broadgate and Cross Cheaping. The fruit and vegetable market was given a new home in 1922 when the city council took over the army barracks. Retail trade took place from stalls in the centre of the old parade ground and other army quarters became home for various wholesale firms. The West Orchard market off Cross Cheaping, near the blitzed market hall, closed in 1953 and transferred to an area of derelict land off Corporation Street. It was called Rex market after the cinema which stood on the site. The Barracks and Rex markets were finally brought together in November 1958 when the new circular market opened. This photograph shows how Market Square looked in 1905. On the left is the fish market, and opposite it is the hotel which later became the Market Tavern. The street running across the back is West Orchard.

Saturday shoppers making their last purchases in the West Orchard market before it transferred to the Rex site in 1953.

Coventry market was invaded by thousands of shoppers determined to make the most of the last Saturday before Christmas in 1964. Crowds gather round the outdoor stalls looking for a bargain.

Inside the market shoppers throng around the stalls of F.A. Harridence; Buddy Doyle, the nylon specialist; Bambrick's; and C. Whatsize & Sons.

Coventry retail market celebrated its twenty-first birthday on 7 November 1979 with the cutting of a huge cake and sherry all round. The cake, baked in the shape of the market building, was cut by Arthur Frith, the president of the National Market Traders' Federation. It was later handed over to the children's wards at the Gulson hospital and the Coventry and Warwickshire hospital by Councillor Harry Richards, the Lord Mayor of Coventry. Thirty of the 169 traders at the market had been there since Princess Alexandra opened it in 1958. At the front, from left to right are: Arthur Frith, Pamela Hayling the nursing officer at Gulson Hospital paediatric unit and, wearing his chain of office, the Mayor, Councillor Harry Richards.

Opposite above: One of Coventry market's best-loved characters, pictured in 1974, was seventy-year-old Emma Chapman – Pem to her friends. At this time, she was having to call it a day due to failing eyesight. Pem's plump and cheery figure had been a familiar sight in the city centre for over forty years but sadly she had recently been informed that it was too late to do anything to improve her sight. She said 'I want to keep on with the flowers for as long as I can'.

Opposite below: Manageress Marie Harris and her colleague Bonnie Chinn dish out the tripe at the Hayes stall in Coventry market in January 1979. Lancashire lad George 'Tripey' Hayes established G.H. Hayes & Co. in Coventry just after the First World War. He had moved to the city to work in the munitions factories and, not happy with the way he was served his tripe in the Midlands' style of steaming liquid, he set up his own shop to sell tripe the cold Lancastrian way. Tripe is, of course, the lining of a bullock or cow's stomach and undergoes many processes including washing, overnight soaking, grading, rough stripping, bleaching and brushing before going on sale in the shops.

Coventry became the centre for a Sunday market war in 1976 with two huge rival markets battling for the same customers. This picture shows hundreds of shoppers at the Fiesta public house site in Longford Road. A Nottinghamshire market promotions company had organised fourteen Sunday markets with 300-400 stalls. A rival firm from Ruislip had already announced that they would be holding a 200 stall market in the city centre. Both companies were keeping their locations a secret. To get around Sunday trading laws, shoppers paid 5p in club membership to get into the Fiesta pub grounds. Stallholders were also club members and as they were selling to each other, were legally selling to club members rather than the public.

three

Last Orders

The Craven Arms Hotel in the High Street was a commercial and posting house, and a Mitchell's and Butler's house in 1880 when the era of coaching had come to an end. It had a reputation for comfort and moderate charges and was popular with passengers on their long and often difficult journeys. It was called the Bear until 1668, the White Bear from about 1773 and became the Craven Arms in around 1811. It had a new mock Tudor frontage by the 1920s but was finally demolished in 1980 to make way for new bank premises. This photograph dates back to the early 1900s. On the wall of the premises to the left is a poster for Louis Tussauds' Grand Tableaux Waxworks featuring Dr Crippen, Mrs Crippen, Miss LeNeave, Williams the master murderer, Mrs Seddon and Miss Barrow. In the hotel's cobbled entrance are billboards advertising properties for sale, lease and rent.

When hotheads in the centre of Coventry wanted to settle a quarrel back in the 1930s, they were told to 'go up to Sproul's'. The Sproul family ran a pub called the O Rare Ben Johnson (thought to have been built on a spot that Ben Johnson had once stood) in New Street, and there was a boxing ring in the backyard. It was the venue not only for those with grudges but also for those who fancied themselves with the boxing gloves. Every Sunday would see free bread and cheese laid out for pensioners, and members of the Three Spires Angling Club (which used the pub as its headquarters) would make part of their catch available on the covered bagatelle table. The fishing club was one of the finest in the country, one of its members being Billy Lane who was to become World Champion. Both New Street and the O Rare Ben Johnson have now gone along with four other licensed premises in the road: the Britannia, the Irish Club, the White Bear and the Livery Stables. Now the area is buried under the Coventry Lanchester polytechnic.

Above: The White Lion in Smithford Street in 1950 was the last building to be demolished to make way for the Upper Precinct. Mary Smith lived at the White Lion in the late 1930s when her father, John Lunn, was the publican. She recalled that 'the pub had a beautiful interior, the large bay window being the public bar. To the right was a passageway to the main entrance, a smoke room, kitchens, and a staircase to the Grosvener function room and restaurant. The large window in the centre of the first floor was our private lounge with a view across the street to the city's arcade, Selfridges, and Woolworths.'

Right: The Canal Tavern in Leicester Row in 1963. The licensee at that time was Dennis McCallum.

Opposite above: Broken glass and boarded windows at the empty Mermaid Inn in Gosford Street, shortly before its demolition in 1967.

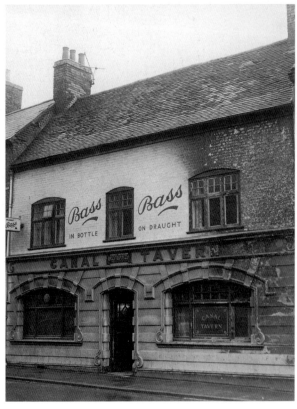

Above: Part of the frontage and a few broken windows were all that remained of the Bear Inn in the High Street in December 1980. Workmen had been knocking down the mock-Tudor public house for over a month to make way for a new branch of Barclays Bank, the construction of which was due to be started in early 1981. Tiles and other materials from the Bear were bought by the city council to use in the repair of older properties including the Council House and St Mary's Hall.

A landmark disappearing: demolition work begins on the White Lion Public House at Gosford Green in 1987. The building had to be pulled down as part of the Far Gosford Street relief road schemes.

The White Lion pub which had helped to quench the thirst of Coventry drinkers for over a century left passers-by with a dry throat as it crumbled. Dust billowed across the Walsgrave Road as the sandstone blocks of the old building succumbed to the demolition men. With them went a slice of the city's football history; back in the 1880s, players from the Singer's club, later to become Coventry City FC, used the back room for changing before sprinting across the road to play their match.

Sunshine and smiles from pensioners and regulars at the Windmill public house in Spon Street on their way to board a coach for the Cotswolds on their annual outing in August 1973.

A group of regulars outside Spon End's Black Horse, one of Coventry's oldest and most popular pubs, saddened by its imminent demolition. The Black Horse was razed to the ground in 1989 as part of a £1.3 million improvement scheme for the busy Spon End and Hearsall Lane junction. The 250-year-old pub attracted customers from as far as Tile Hill, Chapelfields and Canley and was highly regarded for the quality of its draught beers. One customer who had used the pub for thirty years said: 'they can't knock it down. It's the best pint in the country.'

Right: The Dun Cow in Jordan Well prior to demolition in 1968.

Below: Another pub under threat was the M&B owned Black Horse. It dated back some 200 years and a fight was on to save it from the £4 million widening of the Butts into Spon End. The Black Horse used to be the headquarters of a pigeon club founded in nearby Craven Street which included well-known pigeon fanciers such as George Howe, David Ingram, Albert Jones and the 'Snowy' Crowton family.

four

On the Rails

Coventry station in 1869. This picture shows a 2-2-2 'Bloomer' and a DX 0-6-0 hauling a goods train. The complete exposure of the driving wheel earned the Bloomer its nickname after a contemporary fashion in ladies' dress.

Coventry station in 1905, shortly after the reconstruction of the upside. The footbridge at the end of the station was later replaced by one immediately behind the luggage bridge in the foreground. A 'Cauliflower' 0-6-0 is entering the station.

Passengers wait on a crowded platform for the arrival of their train in 1956. In 1935, the Mayor, Alderman T.E. Friswell complained that the down platform was only 15ft wide for a considerable distance and, at 185 yards, was far too short to accommodate many of the trains. A complete rebuild with two island platforms was a minimum requirement. He went on to say that he knew of no other town on the system that had such growth as Coventry (the population was 52,000 in 1891 and 190,000 in 1935) but maintained such an antiquated station. His remarks probably resulted in a decision by LMS to enlarge, modernise and improve the station at a cost of £80,000. However, there were delays and war broke out. The post-war scheme became permanently pigeonholed.

Opposite above: Air raid damage to the station in 1940.

Opposite below: This June 1958 picture shows the original Midland Railway locomotive shed that stood at the end of the Birmingham-bound platform. The shed closed in 1923 and was then used as a workshop. Standing just outside it is one of the two original LNWR signals left in the area at that time and, nearer to the camera, a venerable water column dating back to the dawn of railways, built by Edward Bury, a pioneer railway engineer.

The £1 million reconstruction of Coventry railway station gets under way in 1959 with the preparation of the site for the new parcels depot. In the foreground are the concrete outlines of one of the three sidings and, on the right, the depot's concrete entrance to be used as the station's passenger entrance.

An old railway carriage in position on the platform at Coventry station in September 1959. It was used as a temporary waiting room to replace the brick building that was being demolished.

The temporary entrance to the station in use in October 1959. The original entrance had already been demolished.

Roof girders being lifted into place on the skeleton of the main entrance hall at the new station in April 1960. The building, sited at the junction of Park Road and Eaton Road, was to have a concourse – a hall where ticket offices and other facilities would be sited – as well as a meeting place for passengers.

A view from Stoney Bridge of the extensive track re-laying, which was nearing completion in March 1961.

Opposite above: A fifty-ton steam crane was needed to unravel this problem at Coventry station in November 1959. It caused considerable inconvenience to passengers using through trains to and from Birmingham and the north of England. The derailed parcels coach was being used to ferry parcels between platforms during the reconstruction of the station. The locomotive is an ex-LMS Stanier 2-6-2 tank.

Opposite below: Bays of the new parcel depot rise above the old buildings on platform one.

Train spotters were delighted to see the Royal Scot crack express, drawn by the City of Coventry, re-routed from the Trent Valley line in October 1959.

Royal Scot Class 46140 about to leave Coventry with a London express in 1960. The 'Midlander' was very much part of the daily scene.

As the redevelopment of Coventry station neared its final stages, workmen began the demolition of the two houses in Warwick Road previously occupied by the stationmaster and district inspector. Much of the site would be used for the pedestrian-only entrance to the station and the multi-storey car park.

Wyman's shop and the waiting rooms along platform one, pictured shortly before demolition in March 1962. The roof of the new parcels building can be seen towering over the remains of the old buildings in this photograph from 1962.

A view of the new Coventry station seen from flats at the side of the Warwick Road bridge on 27 April 1962. The old station with its dreary, dismal buildings designed to serve a population of 50,000, finally disappeared amid criticism which had extended over fifty years.

Looking down platforms one and two at the station on 27 April 1962. The new station, four times the size of its predecessor had platforms capable of catering for nineteen-carriage trains compared with the eight carriages in the past. Altogether, some 40,000ft of platform space had been provided.

Foleshill station in October 1960. The prize-winning gardens were located to the right of the photograph, by the lamppost. By 1963, Dr Beeching's chief proposal affecting Coventry was his plan to end passenger services on the Nuneaton–Coventry–Leamington line, and close all the intermediate stations. Foleshill would be one of those closed as a result. It was felt that the diminishing use of this station and the bus services covering the main points along the route made it both uneconomic and unnecessary.

Opposite: The gardens at Foleshill station were awarded fifth prize in the 'best-kept station garden' competition in the 1959 Rugby district of British Railway's London Midland region. In 1961, Foleshill won the first-class prize. Stationmaster R.A. Palmer said 'so far as I can remember, the station has not had a first-class prize before, at least not during the last eight years I've been here.' The station garden featured the name 'Foleshill' in flowers and bordered with white stones.

Left: The closing of this small access gate to Foleshill station was strongly criticised by employees of the British Railways Piston Ring Co. Their spokesman said that workers from Nuneaton had to leave by the main entrance, climb a number of steps, cross Lockhurst Lane bridge and descend on the other side. British Railway said it was a safety issue because many people dashed across the line here, residents used it as a short cut and children played on it.

Below: The Lockhurst Lane bridge on the left of the picture which passengers and pedestrians had to use instead.

This derelict site was all that remained of the former Foleshill station in April 1987.

Canley Halt level crossing on 17 September 1964. A pedestrian and traffic census is being carried out with a view to either replacing the old footbridge with a new one, as it was in poor condition, or introducing wicket gates for pedestrians. As a check was being made on pedestrian flow, it was decided to incorporate a traffic census at the same time.

A Coventry Corporation bus crashed through the level crossing gates at Canley on 7 February 1970, just minutes before the 7.45 London-Birmingham express was due. The no. 18 bus was on an outward journey and, according to the conductor Mr C. Cook, was already on the crossing when the gates started to close. The bus collided with the far gate and demolished it. There were no injuries among the passengers, nor to the driver, Mr Cavanagh.

five

Hold Tight
Please

Above: Senior citizens still speak with great feeling about the trams that once rocked and rumbled through the city streets. They never made a loss in operation although the profit was frequently insufficient to meet the heavy loan charges after municipalization. Local people loved them. The Coventry Electric Tramways Co. carried out electrification on the route to Bedworth during 1895 and the first tram ran from Foleshill depot to Coventry station on 5 December. The city was one of the first municipalities to have electric traction and their very own generating plant at Priestley's Bridge provided power. This picture in Broadgate around the turn of the last century shows one of the early electric trams about to move off in the direction of the railway station. This tramcar was supplied by Brush of Loughborough and has garden seats for twenty-six passengers on the upper deck.

Opposite above: When the men of Coventry marched off to war, a huge gap was left in the labour force and appeals went out to the women of the city to help. In June 1915 the *Coventry Herald* declared 'Women of Coventry responding to their country's call'. Among the pictures was one taken of the first group of women conductresses for the local tramcars. Mrs Greenway, pictured here with her driver, was one of those early volunteers. The tram carries a white diamond on a dark background, the route symbol of the Foleshill services. They ran from Coventry station to Bedworth; Broadgate to Foleshill depot; Broadgate to Foleshill by the New Bridge Inn; and Broadgate to Longford.

Opposite below: This smartly turned-out conductress on No. 26 in Eaton Road is thought to be the very first woman who worked on the trams during the First World War.

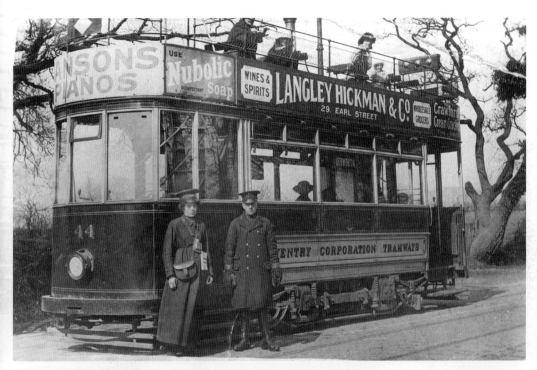

Flags, other decorations and hundreds of coloured lights made this illuminated tram a big attraction as it made nightly trips along Coventry tramway routes shortly before Christmas 1922. The Mayor of the day was appealing for support for his Christmas fund.

Work on the tram lines in Broadgate in the 1930s.

A lovely photograph showing the late night tramcars with their lights blazing on their way up Broadgate in 1936.

A network of tramlines on the road, pictured in 1963, are a reminder of all that was left of the Coventry Corporation tram depot at Foleshill, here almost completely demolished.

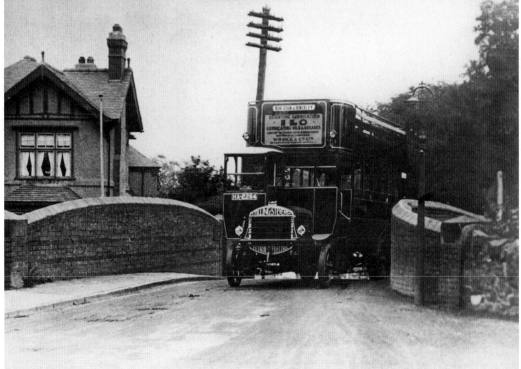

Above: Passengers queue to board a Coventry Transport AEC at the Longford and Bedworth stop in Broadgate during the Second World War. Note the covered headlights on the bus.

Right: A new form of fuel was tested for the city's buses during the war. This was the first Coventry Corporation bus converted for use with a gas-producer trailer. The Corporation transport department was required by the Ministry of War's transport division to convert twenty vehicles to run on gas for use on its passenger services.

Opposite above: Coventry Corporation transport bus fleet, including three new closed-top buses, in 1920.

Opposite below: In the early 1920s, the Midland Red Co. had about 225 vehicles; while Birmingham remained the centre of operations, the Midland Red route map indicated considerable activity in many other Midland towns. The picture shows a Tilling-Stevens Petrol Electric open topper on Coventry Road at Wharfe Bridge in Nuneaton in about 1925.

No crews were available to work on these Corporation buses, parked up at the side of the Burges on 17 September 1962. Coventry bus services were disrupted by a seven-day overtime ban caused by the busmen's protest against the Transport Committee's rejection of their claim for an incentive bonus scheme. The ban reached its peak between 4 p.m. and 6 p.m. each day and caused delays in getting schoolchildren and factory workers home. The buses are two of a fleet of forty Daimlers purchased during 1951-52. They had Daimler engines and were renowned for their smooth quiet operation.

Pictured in December 1966, the Midland Red buses are using the new Pool Meadow bus bays built on the site of the old Coventry Baths in Priory Street, after the Baths had recently been demolished. Nos 586 to Wolston, and 584 to Rugby seen in the centre of the picture are Midland Red S 14s. The bus was a revolutionary design, having lightweight plastic panelling. It seated forty-four passengers and only had single rear wheels.

six

Fire Service

Firemen pose for the camera in the early 1900s in Vicar Lane, off Smithford Street. The brigade have their backs to Smithford Street, with the rear of the Empire theatre to the right of the picture. The brigade captain was Harry Howell who is seated in the centre of the front row.

The Coventry fire brigade with their horse-drawn engines during an inspection in 1911 – exactly fifty years after its foundation. They are pictured outside the former central fire station in Hales Street. The Coventry fire brigade (allegedly the second oldest in the country) was formed in 1861 as a volunteer service with its headquarters in St Mary Street. The volunteer force became semi-professional in 1898 and four years later moved into the Hales Street premises, built in 1902 at a cost of £6,850. The force became totally professional from 1 April 1934.

Firemen pose with their new Daimler motor appliance in 1915, one of the first in the city. The Daimler brigade was proud of the fact that they were the 'first turn-out', even ahead of the city brigade for a local fire. They were ahead too in having four full-time firemen while the city was making do with volunteers.

Hales Street fire station in 1963 with its fleet of Dennis fire engines, ready for any emergency in the city. It was at this time that the 'cramped position' of the fire station was being referred to by Councillor G.W. Sheridan, the chairman of the Waterworks and Fire Brigade Committee. He urged Coventry city council planners to move as quickly as possible to provide a new site for the fire station as the current site was totally inadequate.

Left: New uniforms for the Coventry fire brigade in 1965. Fireman T. Hitchcock, on the left, wears the old uniform, and Fireman W. Howard, on the right, wears the new fire-fighting rig.

Below: The crumbling interior of Coventry's old fire station in Hales Street in April 1992 when the land was being cleared for the new Pool Meadow complex. The handsome old building, built in 1902, was to be retained. The station was in use until 1976 when the fire service moved to Radford Road. The building stood empty for four years and then became an indoor market, a storehouse and a centre for unemployed youngsters.

seven

An Evening Out

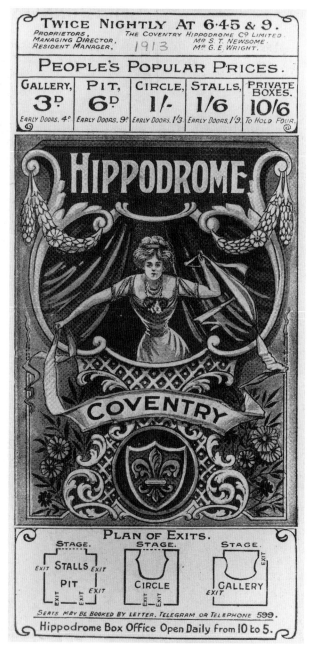

On the programme at the Coventry Hippodrome on
Monday 29 September 1913 were Nellie Boden a 'refined
comedienne and dancer'; Harry Claff, an 'operatic novelty';
and Mina Bax, the 'artistic dancing girl'. Thornley's
Ales were on sale at one shilling and two-pence – for a
gallon jar!

The original Hippodrome of S.T. Newsome, built on the old rope walk in Hales Street, pictured in the 1930s. On Saturday 30 October 1937, it staged its last show, a variety bill featuring Tommy Handley and Joe Young.

On the Monday following the last performance at the old theatre, the New Hippodrome, which had been built alongside it, was opened by the then Mayor of Coventry, Alderman Barnacle. Sam Herbert Newsome owned the theatre. He was known as S.H. and already ran an established motor business. Gillie Potter compèred the first show and artists included Harry Roy and his band. Both the old and new buildings can be seen in this photograph. The New Hippodrome is nearing completion with fencing still in place and a workman precariously balanced at the top of his ladder over the new sign. In the background, looking very run down, is the old Hippodrome.

Audiences travelled from far and wide making Sam Newsome's Coventry Hippodrome the showplace of the Midlands. After television arrived in the 1950s, Sam often said there was nothing to replace the thrill of a packed theatre, but he knew television competition was here to stay. Season after season he brought the stars of the small screen into the Hippodrome. In this 1966 photograph, a coach full of theatregoers from Birmingham arrives to see *The Temperance Seven*.

Opposite above: Opening night of *Puss in Boots* at the Coventry Theatre in Christmas 1962. In the forefront, pictured from left to right, are Frankie Howerd, Sam Newsome (in suit and tie), Sid James and Pauline Grant (holding a bouquet).

Opposite below: The *Puss in Boots* pantomime stars in full voice as they record the Coventry City FC song in December 1962. Jimmy Hill is assisting at the tape recorder.

COVENTRY THEATRE
HALES ST. COVENTRY

TELEPHONE 23141 2 3

HOWARD & WYNDHAM
By arrangement with Dorothy Solomon
Associated Artists Ltd
present

Wed March 20th FOR 8 WEEKS
Mon to Fri 7.30 Sat 5.0 & 8.0
(Also Easter Monday
April 15th at 5.0 & 8.0)
Mats Wed & Thur 2.30
(No Mat Wed April 17th)

THE

BACHELORS

in the

1968 SPRING SHOW

featuring

THE KAYE SISTERS

LUCKY LATINOS
MIKE NEWMAN
JOHNNY HART

SIXTEEN TILLER GIRLS

MIKE YARWOOD

THE GUYS
AND GALS

Directed by
DICK HURRAN

THE GERALDO
ORCHESTRA
under the direction of
PAUL BURNETT

Up to 10,000 costumes were arranged in racks in the wardrobe department of the Coventry Theatre in October 1964. Frances Roe, the wardrobe supervisor seen on the left, holds one of the outfits as her assistant, Eunice Jenkins, checks it.

Opposite: Continuing to support the popular entertainers of the day, this Coventry Theatre poster for the 1968 spring show has The Bachelors as top of the bill along with The Kaye Sisters, with Mike Yarwood at the bottom.

Coventry Theatre moved into the 'push–button age' in January 1967 with the installation of a new stage lighting control system operated at the touch of a fingertip. Costing £20,000, the one-man operated presetting system replaced an old switchboard which needed up to four men to work it. For the theatre's chief electrician, Bert Royale, seen here at the controls, the new equipment ended the heavy labour of working handles which required 56lbs of pressure.

Opposite: Inside the Coventry Theatre in July 1968, the painters are putting the finishing touches to a £20,000 face-lift, working on scaffolding that had been suspended from the ceiling instead of standing on the floor. Hundreds of gallons of paint, more than 5 miles and 28 tons of scaffolding and a month's work had resulted in a brighter, more modern theatre. Audiences would find the walls of the auditorium orange and the proscenium arch midnight blue. Ceilings were in leaf beige. The foyers at the entrance and in the circle were all re-carpeted, as were the six licensed bars and three snack bars. Doors opened again for the first performance of Don Ellis's *Old Tyme Music Hall.*

Workmen tackled a £10,000 facelift at the Coventry Theatre in August 1971. The building was repainted, new steps and a canopy were added to its front entrance, and new electric signs and improved toilets were installed. The work was due to be completed by 6 October that year in time for the birthday show which would star Tommy Steele.

Five young Bay City Rollers fans settle down for a twenty-eight hour wait outside Coventry Theatre in April 1975 to get tickets for the group's concert on 16 May. The tickets were not on sale until 10 a.m. the next day, but the girls were prepared to start their vigil at 7 a.m. the day before to make sure they got tickets at £1.75 each. The girls, from left to right, are: Nada Srbljanin (18), a Henley College catering student who began her wait the day before but gave up because of the bitter cold. When she returned the next day, she was still first in the queue, and reportedly said: 'I would be prepared to pay more than £1.75 to see the Rollers'; Gillian Jones (13) of Tile Hill who said her parents were worried about her staying out all night in the cold but she persuaded them to let her queue; Sue Harris (13) of Allesley Village who had arranged for her parents to deliver hot coffee at intervals through the night; Sue's friends Annette Knight (14) of Highfield, and Denise Kemp (13) of Keresley agreed that not even the near blizzard-like snowstorms of the day before would make them give up their places in the queue.

Protesters gather outside the Coventry Theatre in September 1977 in a bid to prevent the theatre from being turned into a bingo hall. EMI, who owned the theatre, had applied to the Coventry licensing magistrates for a bingo licence.

The Coventry Theatre was to stay open! In a dramatic last-minute move in November 1977, EMI withdrew their application for a bingo licence. Lord Delfont, the chairman and chief executive of EMI, said 'I have always been unhappy about it. I am a theatre man at heart. I had only half-a-dozen letters from members of the public, but what really influenced me was a letter I received from members of the theatre staff.'

The auditorium of the Belgrade Theatre was built by the Coventry Corporation with the aid of timber sent from Yugoslavia, hence the name. The theatre was opened by HRH Princess Marina, the Duchess of Kent, in 1958 and was the first professional theatre to be built in England since the Second World War.

This photograph from March 1958 shows J.C. Brown from the Coventry city architect's department working on a clay model of seventeenth-century Belgrade, from which a concrete cast would be made and placed above the entrance to the Belgrade Theatre. The model was based on a seventeenth-century engraving provided by the Yugoslav Embassy. It was 10ft long and 7ft 6in high with lettering in Slav script for the name of the city.

One of the dressing rooms in the new Belgrade Theatre. There was provision for a company of about thirty-four players.

The Belgrade Theatre in May 1968. The production playing that week was *A day in the death of Joe Egg* by Peter Nicholls.

Above: The 924-seat Globe Picture Theatre first opened its doors in September 1914. In this photograph from the 1920s, the big attraction would be *Pay Day* starring Charlie Chaplin. For a publicity stunt, four of the local lads would dress up and do Chaplin imitations on the cinema steps to attract people in. The boys then joined the manager in a Bullnose Morris for an advertising tour around the city.

Right: The Globe in 1958. Victor Motion Pictures, headed by Oscar Deutsch who started off the better-known Odeon Cinema circuit, took over the Globe in 1925. It then came into the hands of the Philpot circuit, and then the 5 Star Circuit in 1935, before going back to the Odeon circuit, which refurbished it in the early 1940s. At the time of this photograph, there were plans to turn the building into the Majestic Ballroom.

Above: The old standard cinema at the junction of the A45 and Tile Hill Lane in 1939.

Left: A photograph of the Empire cinema taken, 17 February 1961.

Above: Coventry's Paris cinema was built in 1912 in Far Gosford. Showing on 7 March 1958, was *Her Crime was Love* (certificate X), starring Eva Bartok, and *The Diary of Major Thompson* (certificate X), with Jack Buchanan and Martine Carol.

Left: The run down and neglected former Paris cinema in November 1986, five years after its closure in 1981, and after several schemes to reopen it as a leisure complex had fallen through. One small Co-operative had spent two years working on a plan to adapt the cinema into a 300-capacity auditorium, dance hall, bar and café, but the abolition of West Midlands county council meant that no cash was available. The latest project at this time was to develop the site into a multi-cultural shopping and leisure complex.

William Edkins, the manager of the Continental cinema in Earlsdon, was planning a new venture. He wanted to turn La Continentale, which had been showing foreign language films for ten years, into a members-only cinema club with a licensed bar. The seating was to be halved from 400 to 200 to enable a bar lounge to be constructed in the stalls. The club would be called the Moulin Rouge and rules would be strict. Members were to be paid up forty-eight hours before they would be permitted in, and could bring in only two guests each day; they could use the club separately but if they wanted to see a film they would have to pay. The doors would not be open to the public.

Hundreds of would-be first nighters were disappointed when they were turned away from Coventry's newest luxury cinema, the Forum, when it opened in Walgrave Road on Thursday 1 November 1934. After a fanfare of trumpets and the singing of the National Anthem, Gene Gerrard, a popular screen actor of the day, performed the opening ceremony. Also on stage were other personalities from the film world, including Paul Graetz and Margurite Allen who appeared in the film *Blossom Time* at the top of the bill on that day. The Forum closed on 26 May 1962 with the Doris Day film, *Lover Come Back*. A scheme to convert the building into a supermarket, ten-pin bowling alley and ten shops had been put to the planning and redevelopment committee of Coventry city council by a London property development company.

'Fantastic' price paid for Coventry site! The old Opera House site covering about one-third of an acre, in Hales Street, the first freehold site to be sold in the city centre for many years, changed hands for a sum in excess of £100,000 in July 1961. It was the highest price ever paid in the country for such a development, and was in excess of Regent Street, London, prices. Buyers of the site, which had a 70ft frontage, were the dry-cleaning firm of Sketchleys. Planning permission had been granted for the construction of two shops, a dry-cleaners processing plant, and a despatch and receiving depot.

The closure of the Savoy in Radford Road in June 1962 marked the end of the suburban cinema empire of two former Coventry builders, George and Harold Philpot, who at one time operated a total of eight cinemas in the city. The Savoy was the last of the brothers' cinemas to close down. It was generally recognised as one of the best-designed cinemas in Coventry. Built in 1938, it could seat 1,300 people and boasted a very large foyer area. One of its greatest assets was the small Wurlitzer organ, which was once used for BBC broadcasts, bought at a cost of £2,000. It was sold as scrap. Plans had been put forward to convert the site into a supermarket and bowling alley.

The former Tivoli cinema in Webster Street was about to be demolished in September 1980 to make way for a 13,000ft² Co-op supermarket. Mr Henderson, who during children's viewings would threaten to 'cut 12ft off the end of the film' if they did not make less noise, owned the cinema at one time. Not used as a cinema for many years, the Tivoli had been a skating rink, a furniture warehouse and, under the name of Webster Street Studio, the home of the Wheatsheaf players' productions.

Above: In the Locarno Ballroom, no detail for the personal comfort of dancers had been overlooked. The owners wished to give Coventry something 'equal to any fashionable West End hotel'. The ballroom would be run on club lines, and facilities provided in the Stag Room would include shaves, trouser-pressing and shoe-shines, all of which would be free of charge. The ladies' powder room in the above picture had mirrors, each with its own bracket light and a shelf for cosmetics. There was also a depository for leaving handbags in safekeeping.

Opposite above: Dancing at the GEC ballroom.

Opposite below: The heyday of the Locarno Ballroom in the 1960s. Opened in August 1960 by the Mayor of Coventry, Alderman H. Stanley, the Locarno was described as the finest ballroom in Europe. The hall could accommodate 2,500 people and it was the Mecca Ltd policy to use the ballroom every night of the week – teenagers would hold their events on Mondays, old time dances were enjoyed on Tuesdays, over 21s were welcomed on Wednesdays, general dances would take place on Thursdays, private organisations could use the venue on Fridays, palais dances were held on Saturdays and club members alone could make use of the hall on Sundays. The 66ft dance floor was made of Canadian Maplewood and was dominated by the press-button electrically-operated revolving stage from which non-stop dancing would be provided by two bands playing in turn. Coffee tables equipped with table lamps sat on balconies overlooking the dance floor, and there were Tudor Bars, a cocktail bar with leather quilted bar counters and hidden lighting, whereas The New Yorker buffet bar and the long bar were constructed in timber to give a log cabin effect. The impressive lighting system comprised 5,000 bulbs and a vast control room to operate the various lighting plots. Additionally 1,000 small blue stars had been fixed to the ceiling in various star formations, including the Plough, the Bear and the Milky Way.

Left: A helping hand is being given to eighteen-year-old Pam Swindells from Liverpool by Coventry-based professional dancer Barbara Mace at the first British Rotary International Ballroom Dancing Championship at Tiffany's on 8 January 1978. Barbara helped to organise the event and provided recorded music when the band failed to turn up. The event produced an international final round with three couples from Australia, one from South Africa, one New Zealand and two from Britain. The winners were Geoff and Olive Bailey of Bristol.

Right: A family affair at the Rotary dance championships, with Kay Terheege, seen on the right of the picture, and her sixteen-year-old daughter Karen, on the left, both from Wyken in Coventry. In the centre is Kay's daughter-in-law Rachel Terheege of Stoke Golding in Nuneaton.

Opposite: Young ballroom dancers in August 1975. Seen with his regular partner, ten-year-old Wendy Callan from Earlsdon, Craig Morris (also ten years old) from Bell Green in Coventry already had twenty-four trophies and medals to his credit. At the time of this picture, they had recently been presented with gold bars to add to their gold medals for ballroom dancing achievements.

The youngest couple taking part in the Rotary championships in 1978 were Martin Bagburst (16) and Debbie Dolan (15), both of Tamworth.

Young dancers in the Latin American section of the championships at Tiffany's. Karen Newby (16), of Potters Green, Coventry is seen her with her partner Toni Goodwin (17), of Bugbrooke in Northampton.

Other local titles published by Tempus

Buildings of Coventry
GEORGE DEMIDOWICZ

The buildings featured in this book cover almost a millennium of Coventry's history. There are one thousand statutory and locally listed buildings in the city and many of these are splendid examples of their period. This book describes and illustrates some of the finest examples that can be seen today and will serve as a useful guide for those wishing to explore and learn more about the city's history through its buildings.
0 7524 3115 3

Coventry City FC 100 Greats
GEORGE ROWLAND

Over 6,000 players have proudly worn the colours of Coventry City since the club was first formed as Singers FC back in 1883. This volume offers a retrospective look at 100 of the finest players to have represented the club, with a detailed examination of their time at Coventry and their careers in football.
0 7524 2294 4

Nuneaton Volume II
PETER LEE

This selection of over 160 archive images highlights some of the changes and events that have taken place in the town of Nuneaton during the last century. From glimpses of working life in some of the light industries through to the development and modernisation of the town during the 1950s and '60s, each image recalls the social history of Nuneaton.
0 7524 3242 7

Warwickshire CCC 100 Greats
ROBERT BROOKE

Since Warwickshire's first and only bona fide cricket club was formed at Leamington Spa's Regent Hotel on 8 April 1882, it has enjoyed a chequered record of success and failure. There can, however, be no argument about the individual ability of the players who have represented the club over the decades. This volume looks back and recognises the achievements of the men whose contributions made the county.
0 7524 2180 8

If you are interested in purchasing other books published by Tempus, or in case you have difficulty finding any Tempus books in your local bookshop, you can also place orders directly through our website
www.tempus-publishing.com